The Ingredients of
MUSIC

Elizabeth Sharma

Wayland

First published in 1995 by Wayland (Publishers)
Ltd, 61 Western Road, Hove, East Sussex,
BN3 1JD

© Copyright 1995 Wayland (Publishers) Ltd

Editors: Louise Woods and Cath Senker
Design: Joyce Chester
Illustration: Tony de Saulles
Consultant: Valerie Davies, teacher and adviser
for Primary and Special Music, East Sussex

**British Library Cataloguing in Publication
Data**
Sharma, Elizabeth
Ingredients of Music
I Title II Saulles, Tony de
781.2
ISBN 0 7502 1592 5

Typeset by Joyce Chester
Printed and bound by B.P.C. Paulton Books,
Britain

Acknowledgements
The publishers would like to thank the following
for allowing their pictures to be reproduced in
this book:

AKG, London: cover, top right; Bridgeman Art
Library: 6; Camera Press: 28 bottom (Ray Green);
Chapel Studios: cover, main picture (Zul
Mukhida), 7 (Tim Richardson), 11 bottom, 27
(Jayne Knights); Life File: cover, top middle
(Jeremy Hoare), 28 top (Nicola Sutton); Northern
Picture Library: 18, 25; Panos: cover top left
(Victoria Keble-Williams), cover middle
(N. Durrell McKenna); Redferns: 10 (Resource
Foto), 20 and 26 top (Odile Noel); Robert
Harding: 5 (Adam Woolfitt), 11 top; Topham:
22, 23; Wayland: contents page & 8 (APM
Studios), 9 (Garry Fry), 26 bottom (Zul Mukhida);
Zefa: 12, 14, 17, 21.

Cover pictures: (top left) Gitega drummers,
Burundi; (top middle) folk group, Venezuela;
(top right) French lute player, about 1500;
(middle) man with mouth organ, Zimbabwe;
(main picture) guitar player.

Words in **bold** appear in the glossary on page 30.

Contents

♪ This symbol beside
the text indicates an
activity.

Introducing the ingredients

Think of any piece of music that you like. It may be an orchestral piece, a pop song, a recorder piece that you have learned at school, or a steel band piece.

Think about why you like it and then think how you would describe it to someone who has never heard it.

You could try to sing or whistle the tune (also called the melody) but this may not show exactly why you like the piece. There would probably be quite a lot missing.

When you sing the tune of a piece, you may also remember the harmony, that is, the accompaniment or backing, that you usually hear with the tune. You may recall the beat, or rhythm, too.

You may remember the sound of several other instruments or voices which go with the main melody, making an exciting texture of sound.

You may have noticed the dynamics of the piece, that is, which passages are quiet or loud.

The fact that you remember the tune at all probably means that the main phrases are repeated several times during the piece. This gives it form, or structure.

Next time you hear a piece of music you like, try concentrating on each of these ingredients in turn.

This orchestra brings all the ingredients of music together.

The melody lingers on

This village wedding, painted by Pieter Brueghel (c. 1564–1638), shows peasants dancing to melodies played by bagpipes.

Melody is as old as the human voice. The rise and fall of the voice in speech makes a kind of melody. Singing is just the next step.

Thousands of years ago people worshipped the things that affected their lives – the sun, the moon and the forces of nature. They celebrated the seasons and special events, such as births, marriages and harvests.

♪ Make a list of the events you celebrate, and the songs
♪ or hymns you sing. Melodies make the words easier to
remember and more special. Which can you remember
more easily, a poem or a song?

For thousands of years, the music of ordinary people was just a melody, sometimes accompanied by clapping or drums or other percussion instruments. This is still true today in many parts of the world.

More than two thousand years ago, in the ancient civilizations of China, India, Egypt, Greece and Rome, many different musical instruments were invented. They were mostly played to accompany singing. Sometimes the instrument would copy the voice. The melody was the most important ingredient.

In pop, soul and reggae music, the lead singer sings the melody.

The first steps

Melodies are based on **scales**, but originally scales came from melodies. Scales are musical ladders. They grew out of the notes people sang most often, and the notes which filled in the gaps when the tune jumped about.

Sing *Baa Baa Black Sheep*. Move your hand up and down to match the rise and fall of the tune. Now, play the tune starting on C. Write down all the notes you have used, in letters or on the **stave**, and then arrange them in the order of the scale.

These children are using their hands to show the tune moving up and down the scale, or musical ladder.

You can compose good melodies using the pentatonic scale.

There are many different scales found all over the world. Some of them sound very different from the scale you have just used. There is one scale that is found in India, China, Scotland, Ireland and Africa, and which is also used by the Inuit in northern Canada. It is called the 'pentatonic', or five-note, scale.

♪ Take all the notes off a xylophone except these:

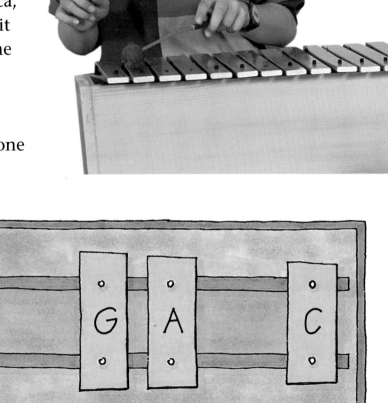

C D E G A C

Play the notes in any order – they will usually make a good melody. Experiment and write down your best tunes. You can work with a partner, both playing different tunes, or one could play two notes at once, making a **chord**, while the other plays a melody.

Indian and Arabic melodies

This Indian woman plays a raga on a stringed instrument called a veena.

In Indian and Arabic music, the melody is the most important ingredient. In both these cultures the melodies are based on very different scales.

Classical Indian music is based on hundreds of different **ragas**. A raga is a cross between a scale and a melody, and musicians, following strict rules, improvise on them. This means they make up the music as they go along. Each raga expresses a particular mood, and is supposed to be played at a certain time of day. The music created will be different each time the raga is played.

See if you can make up a tune using the notes of Bhairav Raga, below.

C   Db   E   F   G   Ab   B   C

In Arabic music, the scales are called **maqam**. Many maqamat (plural) contain intervals of either one or three quarter-tones between the notes. In Western music, major or minor scales use nothing smaller than a semitone, or half-tone.

The aoud is a popular instrument in Arab countries. It has a smooth fingerboard.

You can only find a quarter-tone if you play an instrument with a smooth fingerboard, like a violin, cello or double bass. Pianos and keyboards cannot make quarter-tones.

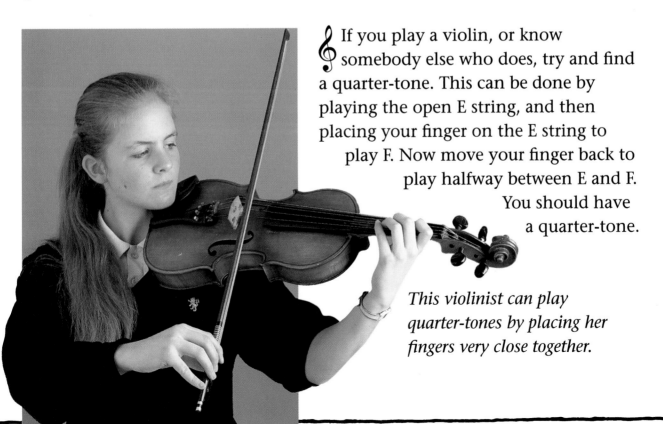

If you play a violin, or know somebody else who does, try and find a quarter-tone. This can be done by playing the open E string, and then placing your finger on the E string to play F. Now move your finger back to play halfway between E and F. You should have a quarter-tone.

This violinist can play quarter-tones by placing her fingers very close together.

Modes and scales

Many ancient plainsong melodies are still sung in churches today.

By the sixth century AD, Christianity had spread all over Europe. Monks chanted the scriptures to different melodies depending on which country they were in. This was because they were influenced by the music of the area, as well as by Jewish and Greek music. In the tenth century, Pope Gregory decided that the same melodies should be used all over the Christian world, and sent messengers all over Europe to make sure this was done.

The melodies were based on **modes**, which are scales made up of only the white notes on a keyboard. Melody based on the modes is called **plainsong**, and it is still used in the Catholic Church today.

The scale most often used in Western music is based on another mode, called the Ionian mode – from C to C. Nowadays this is called a major scale. Western musicians can produce a major scale, with the same pattern of sounds no matter which note they start on, by using sharps and flats.

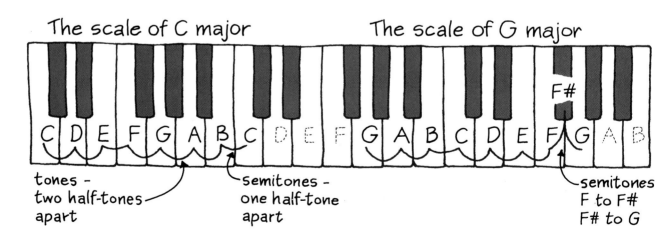

The scale of C major   The scale of G major

F#

C D E F G A B C D E F G A B C D E F G A B

tones –
two half-tones
apart

semitones –
one half-tone
apart

semitones
F to F#
F# to G

Another mode which is used in Western music nearly as often as the major scale, is the minor scale. Play these scales A to A. They have a sadder sound.

The scale of A minor (melodic)

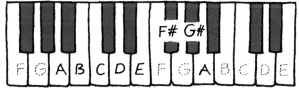

The scale of A minor (harmonic)

The melodic scale has two sharps (F♯, G♯) on the way up, but none on the way down.

Here is a melody for you to play: *Ode to Joy*. This is the theme from Beethoven's *9th Symphony*. It is in the key of G major.

Ode to Joy   **Ludwig van Beethoven**

Whenever you hear a piece of music, try and work out whether it is mainly major or minor. But be careful – many tunes have sections in both types of scale.

The shape of music

Tunes usually follow a pattern of repeated phrases, so that people know what is likely to happen next. A phrase is a short section of music, rather like a sentence in speech. This pattern is called 'structure' or 'form'. People like to join in when well-known songs are sung because it makes them feel they belong to a group. Think about football fans, Guides or Scouts. In order to join in, you need to be able to remember the tune and recognize the phrases that are repeated.

Some of these Spanish folk singers sing phrases with the lead singer. Others clap or play the tambourine in rhythm.

Instrumental music also needs to have a structure, or a shape and pattern, so that the audience can recognize sections of the melody. They can then feel part of the performance even though they are not actually performing. Listeners would lose interest if they could not recognize some features of melody or rhythm to help them remember the music. Composers often use tunes which return at times throughout the piece.

One of the oldest, and still the most popular, musical forms is 'call and response'. In many world religions since ancient times, the leading singer would sing a phrase which would be answered by a phrase sung by the congregation. This still happens to this day. It was also the pattern for the work songs sung by the Africans who were taken as slaves to the southern states of America and the Caribbean. This style developed into the Blues, Jazz and Swing, and influenced all styles of popular music.

Many songs have a chorus which is repeated after every verse. This pattern developed from call and response. This traditional spiritual song has both call and response, and a chorus. It is called *Go Down, Moses*.

Go Down, Moses   **Traditional Spiritual**

Structure and form

Musical forms developed over the centuries because composers, performers and listeners found that certain patterns of musical phrases sounded good. 'Binary' is a word used to describe a two-part form. Here the first melody, A, can be repeated, and then followed by B, which can also be repeated.

Try and play this binary tune. Play section A and then repeat it. Do the same with section B.

Theme from Rosamunde Franz Schubert

'Ternary' form is a three-part form in which the first melody is repeated at the end, after a phrase of different music in the middle. 'Rondo' form introduces more sections which answer or contrast with the first tune.

See if you can work out where to write **A B A C A** in this rondo, *Banana Boat Song*. **A** is the first part, **B** is the second and **C** is the third. Write the letters against the sections of music which are repeats of the first tune or contrasting sections.

Banana Boat Song   **Traditional Work Song**

The musical forms mentioned so far are quite simple and short, but composers developed rules for writing long pieces of music in sections called **movements**. The first movement was usually fast, the second slow, the third in ternary form, and the fourth fast, like the first.

An orchestra rehearses long pieces one section at a time.

Listen to the First Movement of Mozart's *40th Symphony in G Minor* or Beethoven's *5th Symphony in C Minor* and see if you can find any tunes that are repeated.

Rhythm in Western music

The drum rhythm helps the soldiers march smartly in time in this pipe and drum band.

Our lives depend on rhythm. Heartbeat, breathing and speech are all rhythmic. Perhaps this is why the regular beat of a piece of music is called the **pulse**. The **tempo** is the speed of the pulse. Rhythm patterns can be quite simple or very complex, but they are still based on the regular pulse. Rhythm is what makes you want to dance or march to music.

In Western music, rhythm patterns can be written down so that someone who has never heard a piece of music can read it and play it.

Music is divided into bars, separated by bar lines.

At the beginning you can usually find two numbers, one above the other:

$$\frac{2}{4} \qquad \frac{3}{4} \qquad \frac{4}{4} \qquad \frac{6}{8}$$

The lower number is usually 4, but sometimes it is 8 or another number. These numbers tell us the kind of beats we are counting in. Number 4 as the lower number tells us we are counting four beats, or 'crotchets', in each bar. In the USA these are called quarter-notes. They look like this:

$\frac{4}{4}$ means that each bar must have notes to the value of 4 crotchets.

$\frac{3}{4}$ means that each bar must have notes to the value of 3 crotchets.

$\frac{2}{4}$ means there have to be notes to the value of 2 crotchets in each bar.

The first beat of the bar is the most important, so it is often played a little louder. This gives music its regular beat, and makes us want to dance or at least tap our feet.

Work in groups of up to four or five. Decide on your favourite cassette of pop music. It is probably in $\frac{4}{4}$ time, but to make sure, you will have to listen for the strong beat and count.

Each of you choose a percussion instrument with a contrasting sound and make up your own rhythm pattern. It can be just one bar long, or two, or four.

Here is a simple example:

Player 1	Player 2	Player 3	Player 4
♩ ♩ ♩ ♩	♫ ♫ ♫ ♫	𝅗𝅥 𝅗𝅥	𝅝
1+1+1+1=4	$\frac{1}{2}+\frac{1}{2}+\frac{1}{2}+\frac{1}{2}+\frac{1}{2}+\frac{1}{2}+\frac{1}{2}+\frac{1}{2}=4$	2+2=4	4
crotchets	quavers	minims	semibreve

You can make up better patterns than this by mixing up the rhythms, as long as you always make sure there are the right number of beats in each bar.

Play your patterns to go with your cassette. Take it in turns to play, then play together in different combinations to make a piece of music you could play to other people.

Indian and African rhythms

In different parts of the world, rhythm is organized differently. In Indian classical music, there are hundreds of rhythm cycles, just as there are hundreds of ragas. A rhythm cycle, which is called a **tal**, is a fixed number of beats divided into sections called **vibhags**. These are rather like the bars in Western music, except that vibhags are not always the same length. Different tala (plural) have different names, like the ragas. Indian classical musicians must improvise on the tal, as well as on the raga.

Three of these Indian drummers are playing tabla – pairs of drums which can make many different sounds.

The most important beat of the tal is the first, called the **sam** (marked X). The first beat of the other vibhags (marked x) is also important, but one vibhag has to be a contrast. It is called **khali** (and marked O). Khali means 'empty', so it has to be played quietly. Players only use a small drum for the khali.

One tal is called the 'tintal' and has 16 beats, rather like 4 bars in $\frac{4}{4}$ time.

Work with a partner. Choose instruments with contrasting sounds. See if you can compose a rhythm pattern in tintal.

1 2 3 4 | 5 6 7 8 | 9 10 11 12 | 13 14 15 16 |
X   x   O   x
Sam   Khali

You should both play the sam together strongly, but then you can make up your own rhythm pattern to fit into the tintal cycle. The partner with the loudest or lowest instrument should stop for the khali vibhag.

In Africa the people from each area have their own special songs and rhythms for dances. The rhythms are not written down – they must be remembered and passed from one generation to the next. Often the rhythm patterns are very complicated with clapping and stamping as well as drums, rattles and bells.

These Kenyan drummers play for village celebrations.

Harmony around the world

Harmony is the organized sound of two or more notes sounding at the same time. People's opinions about what makes a harmonious sound have changed over the centuries. In medieval Europe, monks liked to sing their plainsong melodies with some monks singing five notes lower than the main choir. This could originally have been because some monks could not sing in tune (or had deeper voices), but it became a tradition. Gradually the third note of the chord was added in some parts of the tune.

By the fifteenth and sixteenth centuries, composers had developed the style of having the tunes played or sung at different times so that melodies

Monks have sung plainsong melodies in the same way throughout the centuries.

seemed to weave in and out of each other. This was called 'polyphony', which means 'many voices'. Listen to any music by William Byrd or Giovanni Palestrina. You can hear chord sounds, but only as the melodies flow through them.

A simple example of polyphony is the **round**, also called the **canon**. You probably know *London's Burning* or *Row Row Row Your Boat*.

Try this Australian round with four groups.
A new group starts from the beginning
each time the first line finishes.

Kookaburra   **Traditional**

Koo - ka - bur - ra sits on the old gum tree____

Mer - ry mer - ry king of the bush is he____

Laugh koo - ka - bur - ra, laugh koo - ka - bur - ra

Gay your life must be.

In Indian classical music the harmony is created by the rise and fall of the melody, played on the **sitar**, or other instruments, which is heard against the continuous **drone** of the **tanpura**. This instrument plays **Sa**, the lowest note of the Indian scale, all the time.

Versions of the bagpipes are played in Scotland, Ireland, Northumbria, in other parts of Europe and in some Arabic countries. A drone sounds all the time as the melody rises and falls in bagpipe music.

This young bagpiper can play melody and drone together.

23

Harmony in Western music

In Western music, most harmony is based on chords which are made from the notes of the scale used for the melody. In its simplest form, a chord consists of three notes, called a **triad**.

This is C major. C is the root, E is the 3rd, because it is the 3rd note of the scale above C, and G is the 5th.

The chord of C major

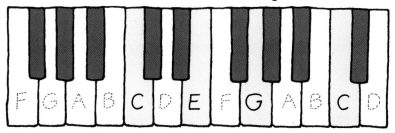

Chords are mostly major or minor. Play these triads and notice how they sound. Which ones sound happy and which ones sound sad?

C	E	G	C major
C	E♭	G	C minor
D	F	A	D minor
D	F♯	A	D major

Now try playing these. Listen carefully and work out which are major and which are minor. Play the three notes together, and then separately so that you can hear each one clearly.

E	G	B	E	G♯	B
F	A	C	F	A♭	C
A	C	E	A	C♯	E

When you play the notes separately, you can play them in various different patterns. These are called **arpeggios**.

C major arpeggios

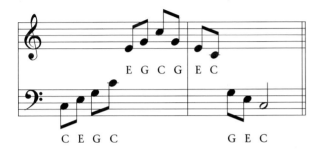

E G C G | E C

C E G C   G E C

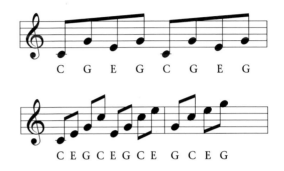

C   G   E   G   C   G   E   G

C E G C E G C E   G C E G

Try playing some of the chords on page 24 as arpeggios.

The chords and the way they are played help create the mood of a piece of music. Play them in different moods, by playing loud, soft, as arpeggios and at different speeds.

It is possible to harmonize the same tune in several different ways. To harmonize a tune you pick out the most important notes in each bar (usually the 1st, then the 3rd) and find chords which contain that note. Then decide which order of chords sounds best.

You would want to use harsh, clashing sounds if you were composing music about lightning or a storm.

Sometimes composers deliberately choose notes which make a discord – a sound which clashes, to make a dramatic or frightening sound. Listen to Stravinsky's *Rite of Spring* or to *Mars* from Holst's *Planet Suite*.

Texture

The texture of music is the combination of sounds you can hear. Listen to the thin texture of the solo flute and harp at the beginning of Vaughan Williams' *Fantasia on Greensleeves* and then listen to the warmth and thickness as the strings come in.

You learned how to make chords in their simplest form, triads, in the chapter on harmony (see page 24). You can make chords of a thicker texture by doubling all or some of the notes.

The sweet, high sound of the flute can be heard above the whole orchestra.

First play the triad of C major (C E G) on the piano or keyboard, then play the same chord higher or lower on the keyboard. Get a friend to help you and play as many Cs, Es and Gs as you can, all at once.

Now try playing the chord softly, then loudly. Try playing the chords **tremolando** by wiggling your fingers up and down quickly on the keys. Try repeating the chord quickly in a quaver rhythm.

This girl is playing the triad of C minor.

Experiment with playing the chords high and low, softly as a triad, louder with the notes doubled. Try them as arpeggios. Try out all these chords:

D major: D F♯ A   D minor: D F A
E major: E G♯ B   E minor: E G B
F major: F A C   F minor: F A♭ C
G major: G B D   G minor: G B♭ D

Try out all the sounds or 'voices' the keyboard makes. Notice which 'voices' sound best when played at a high pitch, and which sound better played in the medium or low range. Form some triads or chords. Some 'voices' blend well as a triad, or as a thicker, textured chord.

Try using the 'violin' sound together in a thick textured chord, then the 'brass' sounds. Make a list of all the sounds you like the best as solo sounds, or as a thick texture of sound.

Press 'auto chord', 'auto rhythm' or 'single finger', and play a note at the low-sounding end of your keyboard. You will hear a whole chord played as a rhythm. It may sound like a full orchestra or a rock or reggae group.

Press 'style' and try out all the different auto chord rhythms the keyboard will play, from rock to baroque! If you have a switch saying 'small', 'medium' or 'large', play a single-finger chord and compare them. 'Small' usually gives you a bass line and some drumming. 'Medium' is a thicker texture, with simple chords. 'Large' may include a full orchestra, arpeggios, short snatches of melody from various instruments, and a complex texture of sound.

This girl is playing notes at the bass end of her keyboard. Do you think she is playing a melody or a dramatic, clashing sound?

Dynamics

You sometimes speak softly when you are soothing a baby or a pet, or telling someone a secret. You speak loudly when you are excited or angry, and shout when you cheer on sports day, or when warning someone of danger.

Music also has to show contrast between loud and soft, and sometimes it expresses the same emotions that we express in speech. You would not sing a lullaby loudly, or you'd frighten the baby. You would not cheer softly at a football match.

The human voice can be soft, (above) or very loud (below).

In Western music, Italian terms are usually used and understood by musicians all over the world. *Piano* (*p*) means 'quiet' and *forte* (*f*) means 'loud'.

♪ Make a list of some sounds you hear every day at home or at school, and next to them write a suitable dynamic marking.

pp
pianissimo
very quiet

p
piano
quiet

mp
mezzopiano
moderately quiet

mf
mezzoforte
moderately loud

f
forte
loud

ff
fortissimo
very loud

There are other signs which
describe dynamics. *Crescendo*
means 'get louder' and
diminuendo means 'get quieter'.

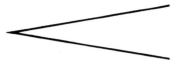

*This is a
crescendo sign...*

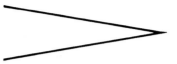

*...and this is a
diminuendo sign.*

Play this Russian tune *Song of the Plains* over and over
again. It is supposed to show an army coming from
far away, getting louder as it passes by, and then fading
again into the distance. Show this with your dynamics.
You may want to have only the main tune playing to
start with, and gradually add in the harmony parts and
change the texture by adding more instruments.

Song of the Plains

Traditional Russian Folk Song

Glossary

Arpeggio A broken chord, played one note at a time.

Canon A piece of music in which a voice or instrument plays a tune, and other voices or instruments start to play the same tune a few bars afterwards.

Chord A group of notes which sound good when played together.

Drone A piece of music in which one or two notes sound all the time while the melody plays.

Khali A vibhag that is played quietly.

Maqam (plural Maqamat) An Arabic scale.

Mode An ancient scale which, if played on a modern piano, would only use the white keys.

Movement A section of a long piece of music.

Plainsong Vocal music, based on the modes. Plainsong is still used in the Catholic Church.

Pulse The regular beat of a piece of music.

Raga A cross between a scale and a melody. Indian music is based on ragas.

Round Another word for a canon.

Sa The lowest note in the Indian scale.

Sam The first beat of a tal.

Scale A step-by-step ladder of musical notes.

Sitar A stringed instrument with a long neck and a rounded body, played in India.

Stave A set of five lines with four spaces in between, used for writing music.

Symphony A musical piece for orchestra in three or four movements.

Tal (plural Tala) An Indian rhythm cycle.

Tanpura An Indian instrument which only plays one low note.

Tempo The speed of the pulse.

Tremolando Playing notes in a chord separately, but quickly, to make a continuous trembling sound.

Triad The basic three notes of a chord.

Vibhag A section of Indian music, similar to a bar in Western music.

Books to read

Birds and Beasts compiled by Sheena Roberts (A & C Black, 1987)
Instruments around the World by Andy Jackson (Longman, 1988)
Live Music! series: *Brass, Keyboards, Percussion, Strings, The Voice, Woodwind* by Elizabeth Sharma (Wayland, 1992–3)

Music by Alan Blackwood (Wayland, 1988).
Musical Instruments by Louise Tythacott (Wayland, 1995)
The Oxford First Companion to Music by Valerie and Kenneth McLeish (Oxford University Press, 1982)

Listening list

Indian and African music, 10, 20
Indian classical music e.g. sitar music by Ravi Shankar, santoor music by Shiv Kumar Sharma, sarod music by Ali Akbar Khan.

Modes and scales, 12
Ode to Joy, the theme from the last movement of the *9th Symphony* by Ludwig van Beethoven.

Structure and form, 16
Rosamunde theme by Franz Schubert.
Symphony Number 40 in G Minor by Wolfgang Amadeus Mozart.
Symphony Number 5 in C Minor by Ludwig van Beethoven.

Rhythm in Western music, 18
Madrigals and church music by William Byrd and Giovanni Palestrina.

Harmony in Western music, 24
The Rite of Spring by Igor Stravinsky.
Mars from *The Planet Suite* by Gustav Holst.

Texture, 26
Fantasia on Greensleeves by Ralph Vaughan Williams.

Dynamics, 28
Dynamic contrasts and textures in *Carmina Burana* by Carl Orff.

Index